W9-CLH-268

Preserving Human Rights Around the World

CHARITY &
PHILANTHROPY
UNLEASHED

Tammy
Gagne

Mitchell Lane
PUBLISHERS
P.O. Box 196
Hockessin, DE 19707

Conquering Disease
Emergency Aid
Environmental Protection
Helping Children with Life-Threatening Medical Issues
Helping Our Veterans
Preserving Human Rights Around the World
The Quest to End World Hunger
Support for Education

PUBLISHER'S NOTE: The facts in this book have been thoroughly researched. Documentation of such research can be found on pages 44–45. While every possible effort has been made to ensure accuracy, the publisher will not assume liability for damages caused by inaccuracies in the data, and makes no warranty on the accuracy of the information contained herein.

The Internet sites referenced herein were active as of the publication date. Due to the fleeting nature of some web sites, we cannot guarantee that they will all be active when you are reading this book.

Printing 1   2   3   4   5   6   7   8   9

Library of Congress Cataloging-in-Publication Data

Gagne, Tammy.
 Preserving human rights around the world / by Tammy Gagne.
      pages cm
 Includes bibliographical references and index.
 ISBN 978-1-61228-574-0 (library bound)
 1. Human rights--Juvenile literature. I. Title.
 JC571.G233 2015
 323--dc23
                                                    2014006924

eBook ISBN: 9781612286129

                                                          PBP

Contents

Introduction 4

CHAPTER 1

THE FIGHT FOR FREEDOM 6

From Snitch to Hero 11

CHAPTER 2

SPEAKING OUT AGAINST CENSORSHIP 12

The Ultimate Price 17

CHAPTER 3

ENDING DISCRIMINATION 18

Women in Rwanda 25

CHAPTER 4

THE IMPORTANCE OF DIGNITY AND EDUCATION 26

Education Helps People Help Themselves 33

CHAPTER 5

ENFORCING HUMAN RIGHTS LAWS 34

The Situation in Syria 41

What You Can Do to Help 42

Chapter Notes 43

Further Reading 44

Books 44

On the Internet 44

Works Consulted 44

Glossary 46

Index 47

Introduction

As Americans, we have heard the term "life, liberty, and the pursuit of happiness" so many times that we may overlook its significance. But when we consider the millions of people around the world who are still fighting for these basic human rights, something amazing happens. We remember just how fortunate we are to have the rights provided by those profound words found in the Declaration of Independence. We also realize how important it is to keep the fight for human rights going.

Certainly, we aren't the only country in the world that respects basic human rights. On December 10, 1948, the General Assembly of the United Nations adopted the Universal Declaration of Human Rights. This document, which has since become a standard reference on the subject, begins by recognizing that "the inherent dignity" and "equal and inalienable rights of all members of the human family is the foundation of freedom, justice, and peace in the world . . ."[1]

Unlike many other international documents, the Universal Declaration of Human Rights is unique in that it is not a treaty. No country is legally bound to follow its guidelines. At the same time, this list has been invoked over and over for more than sixty years as a foundation for human rights laws. It has even served as a model for developing international agreements that are indeed legally binding. Both the International Covenant on Civil and Political Rights, which addresses the rights to freedom of religion and voting, and the International Covenant on Economical, Social, and Cultural Rights, which establishes rights for employment, health care, and education, were shaped from the Universal Declaration of Human Rights.

Even with international agreements like these in place, however, the citizens of the world must remain vigilant. Several countries with problematic human rights records have recently sought seats on the United Nation's Human Rights Council. The leaders of some of these countries have even killed or tortured their own people in order to stay in power. Philippe Bolopion is the United Nations Director for a non-profit group called Human Rights Watch. This independent organization is dedicated to defending and protecting human rights. Bolopion offers, "Syria's candidacy, if maintained, would be a cruel joke, but would almost certainly be met with a resounding defeat. . . . Iran too falls far short of the most basic standards expected of Human Rights Council members and sticks out even in an overall disappointing pool of candidates in the Asia group, with deeply problematic contenders such as Vietnam, China, or Saudi Arabia."[2] Other questionable countries seeking seats include Algeria, Chad, Cuba, and Russia.

The task of securing human rights for all is definitely not an easy one. Getting all of the world's countries to agree on the exact definition of human rights—and what laws should be put in place—is a vast and complicated undertaking. Getting certain countries to adopt and enforce human rights is an even bigger job. But it is one that many organizations think is worth all the time and effort involved.

CHAPTER 1

The Fight for Freedom

What do you think of when you hear the phrase human rights? Do you envision the right to live in a society where everyone is treated as an equal? Does the right to vote or participate in government come to mind? How about the simple right to live as a free person? You have probably read about African American slavery in your history books at school. This horrible practice was a part of our nation's history for many years before it was finally outlawed with the Thirteenth Amendment in 1865. Although slavery is a thing of the past in the United States, it is very much in the present in other parts of the world, like the African country of Sudan.

Ker Aleu Deng was just a young boy when Arab raiders stormed his village in what was then southern Sudan. The invaders killed the men and tied women and children, like Deng and his mother, to camels, dragging them behind. Forced into slavery, Deng worked as a goat keeper on his captor's property. At the end of each day, he was left to sleep outside with the goats like an animal.

To make a horrible situation even worse, Deng's captor was an abusive alcoholic. He would often beat the young boy, but one day the abuse became even more brutal than usual. His captor rubbed juice from hot chili peppers into Deng's eyes. And as if that wasn't enough, he went on to hang the twelve-year-old upside down over a fire. The combination of the pepper juice and smoke from the fire caused Deng to go blind.

A humanitarian group called Christian Solidarity International (CSI) rescued Deng and brought him to the United States in 2011,

Ker Aleu Deng was blinded as a slave in Sudan. After being rescued by Christian Solidarity International, he came to the United States where he met Dr. Julia Haller. Thanks to her, Deng now has his vision back in one of his eyes. Here, doctor and patient are shown at a press conference in 2011, where they spoke about Deng's ordeal. Deng wants the world to know that there are many other people who are still suffering in Sudan. The twenty-two-year civil war between the northern and southern regions of the country came to an end in 2005, when South Sudan won its independence. But many people, like Deng's mother, remain enslaved in the north.

when he was eighteen years old. Eye doctors in the US performed surgery on him at this time. They were unable to save the vision in Deng's left eye. Remarkably, though, he can now see again with his right eye.

Deng and his heartbreaking experience made a big impression on Dr. Julia A. Haller, who managed his treatment. "He is so bright and charming that we all fell in love with him," she says. "We found his story to be just heart-rending. Reading about slavery in the newspaper is one thing, but meeting a blinded slave boy in person is another. Taking on the privilege of [Deng's] care has had a huge impact on everyone on the team. It's been a wake-up experience for all of us."[1]

Although his life is much improved now, Deng says he is still haunted by the years he spent as a slave. "Every single day it plays in my head," he told the House Foreign Affairs Sub-Committee on Africa, Global Health and Human Rights.[2] He testified at a hearing in October of 2011 to help raise awareness in the United States about the problem of Sudanese slavery.

Deng plans to return to his home in what is now officially South Sudan. He also wants to help the people, like his mother, who are still enslaved in Sudan. Sadly, he doesn't know where she is, or even if she is still alive.

John Eibner, chief executive officer of CSI, reports that his organization will keep up their work in this area. "CSI will continue to focus on this problem until the last slave is free," he promises.[3]

It is difficult to say how many people are enslaved in the world today. Experts say that because there's not enough concern for the issue, there is a lack of solid data. It is safe to say that millions of people throughout the world are victims of this and other types of human rights violations. One of the largest groups of people denied basic human rights is women.

In many places today women hold positions of power in both business and politics. Numerous American companies such as Hewlett-Packard, Pepsi, and Williams-Sonoma have female CEOs. Women also have high-level positions in the governments of countries including Senegal, Thailand, and the United Kingdom. Just fifty years ago, however, women didn't have the right to vote in many countries. There are still a few countries that don't offer equal voting rights to women.

Julie Bindel is a British journalist and the co-founder of Justice for Women, an organization that works to stop the abuse of women worldwide. She reveals, "Violence against women is an international epidemic. It has been identified by the World Health Organization as a grave health issue, affecting more people than HIV and AIDS."[4]

Violent acts are committed against women all over the world every day. In some countries, husbands have the legal right to beat or rape their wives. Few women can leave the men who are mistreating them. Even if divorce is allowed by law, poverty or social stigma may keep a woman from leaving her abuser.

Many women in these situations did not choose the violent men to whom they are married. Instead, their families picked their husbands for them. In Pakistan, girls could be married off even before they reach puberty. Their husbands are often cousins they have never met. What happens if a woman falls in love with a man of her own choosing? In Turkey, a male relative has the right to kill a female family member who loves a person whom he considers an unsuitable choice.[5]

Even living in a country whose laws support human rights doesn't guarantee that those laws will be enforced. After a long history of apartheid, South Africa adopted a new constitution in 1996. The document's preamble specifically states that the nation is establishing "a society based on democratic values, social justice, and fundamental human rights."[6] Nonetheless, the number of rapes committed in South Africa is among the highest in the world.

Amnesty International is a leader in the fight for human rights on a global scale. The organization educates people around the world about the importance of human rights for everyone. Presently, the group is working to advance the ratification of an international treaty for the rights of women. It is called the

In some countries women and girls are treated like property, not people. Rasheeda Begum, who lives in Pakistan, was just a year old when her father lost 10,000 rupees (166 US dollars) in a poker game. Since he could not pay his debt, he promised Rasheeda's hand in marriage in place of the money. His opponent, a relative of the family, waited fifteen years to collect on this promise. But he didn't forget. In 2007, he made it clear that he expected Rasheeda to marry him. Above, she and her mother, Nooran Begum, cry together as they tell their story and ask for help in stopping this terrible custom that is still allowed in the country.

Convention on the Elimination of All Forms of Discrimination Against Women (CEDAW). The document has already been ratified by almost all countries—187 out of 194.[7]

Perhaps what is most surprising is that the United States is one of the seven countries yet to ratify the treaty. The others are Iran, Somalia, South Sudan, Sudan, and the Pacific Island nations of Palau and Tonga. In addition to Amnesty International, numerous other organizations support US ratification. They include the American Bar Association, The Leadership Conference on Civil and Human Rights, the NAACP, the National Council of La Raza, National Education Association, and the YWCA.[8]

From Snitch to Hero

Many people assume that the battle for human rights in the United States is a thing of the past. But the truth is that human rights are ever-evolving. Technology in particular has made it necessary to consider human rights from a whole new perspective. When the Universal Declaration of Human Rights was adopted in 1948, there was no such thing as email or cell phones.

In 2013, a twenty-nine-year-old system administrator for the National Security Agency (NSA) packed his bags and boarded an airplane for Hong Kong, China. Around this same time he claimed responsibility for releasing some shocking information to the world. The story involved the NSA's surveillance program. Edward Snowden claimed that the NSA was monitoring phone records and hacking into Internet providers' servers to record emails, photographs, and Internet searches of American citizens, universities, hospitals, and private businesses. He provided copies of official government documents to support his statements.

People all over the world immediately began debating the issue. Was Snowden a traitor to his country for leaking highly classified documents to the press? Or was he a courageous whistleblower for standing up against a terrible violation of human rights? Article 12 of the Universal Declaration of Human Rights states, "No one shall be subjected to arbitrary interference with his privacy, family, home or correspondence, nor to attacks upon his honour and reputation. Everyone has the right to the protection of the law against such interference or attacks."[9]

Daniel Cohn-Bendit and Rebecca Harms are members of the European Parliament who definitely think Snowden is a hero. In September of 2013, the group nominated Snowden for the Sakharov Prize for defending human rights and freedom of thought. Although Snowden did not end up winning the award, the leaders of the group insisted that Snowden "deserves to be honored for shedding light on the systematic infringements of civil liberties by US and European secret services. . . . Snowden has risked his freedom to help us protect ours."[10]

Many people have spoken out in support of Edward Snowden, like these protestors in Chater Garden, Hong Kong.

CHAPTER 2

Speaking Out Against Censorship

Article 19 of the Universal Declaration of Human Rights states, "Everyone has the right to freedom of opinion and expression; this right includes freedom to hold opinions without interference and to seek, receive, and impart information and ideas through any media and regardless of frontiers."[1] The very book you are reading is an example of one of the most important human rights—the freedom of expression. The author used this freedom in writing the words, and you are also exercising it in considering them. You are free to agree or disagree with any opinions contained in these pages, and to share your opinions with others.

Some people will read this book and write reviews about it. A few will even get paid to publish their opinions in magazines or newspapers. Readers who don't review books for a living can still share their opinions. For example, if you purchased this book online, you might leave a customer review on the seller's website. Or you may tell your friends how much you loved or hated it. Whether you find it fascinating, informative, boring, or completely useless, you can say that!

Many people who live in the United States take the freedom of expression for granted. We are able to turn on the television, radio, or computer and listen to news about what is happening in the US, as well as around the world, whenever we like. We can tell others about what we have heard, as well as what we think of it. We can read a news article online and post our own thoughts about the story in the comments section. Others can respond to those thoughts, too. For Americans, accessing news and discussing it freely are such routine activities that they almost

United States First Lady Eleanor Roosevelt helped to raise awareness about human rights on an international level. She is seen in the above photo with Professor Rene Cassin of France presenting the first copies of a guidebook on the subject to Ceylon's Ambassador RSS Gunawardene, chairman of the United Nations Commission on Human Rights. The publication was created in honor of the tenth anniversary of the Universal Declaration of Human Rights. Roosevelt said that the "destiny of human rights" is in the hands of all citizens, and that "it is our hope that this book may inspire them to strengthen their relations with one another..."

seem mundane. But in some parts of the world, people are fighting for this right at this very moment.

One of the biggest barriers to the freedom of expression in several other countries in the Americas is organized crime. In certain countries the government is equally corrupt. Both the criminal organizations and tyrannical governments want to keep the people from hearing or reading news. When the people learn that they aren't the only victims of this type of domination, something drastic happens: The criminals begin losing some of their power.

This change doesn't happen all at once, of course. But gradually, the victims may see that they outnumber the criminals. And once they realize this important fact, they can come together to start solving the problem. Standing up and fighting against organized crime or corrupt governments isn't easy. But it becomes less difficult when the people have access to information about how others around the world have done the same thing. Once oppressed people learn that they aren't alone, they can also reach out for help.

Although many people think that fighting for freedom of expression is worth the cost, it is important to know just how

horrible that fight can be. "More than 260 journalists have been murdered during the first eleven years of this century in Latin America," says Catalina Botero, Special Rapporteur for Freedom of Expression at the Inter-American Commission on Human Rights of the Organization of American States. "The [criminal organizations have] an agenda for the media and when the press doesn't adapt to it, very serious problems can emerge. We are seeing this in places like northern Mexico, Brazil, and in some of the countries of Central America."[2]

Botero points out that "The media is the best ally of justice. When a journalist is killed, it doesn't just affect that person. It keeps a whole community from having access to information that is crucial for exercising political and social control."[3]

Restrictive governments limit freedom of expression by maintaining tight control over the press. In China, this practice is commonplace. Cheng Yizhong is a journalist who helped establish the *Beijing News* in the country's capital city. In 2004, however, he was removed from his position as editor-in-chief of the organization's *Southern Metropolis Daily* newspaper. Along with two other journalists, Yizhong was jailed for more than five months without any formal charges being filed against them. He was eventually released, but barred from reporting in China.

Many people think that Yizhong's "crime" was reporting on controversial issues against the government's wishes. One of his most recent stories had been about the death of a suspect who died while in police custody. Human rights groups applaud Yizhong for speaking out about injustice. The United Nations Educational, Scientific, and Cultural Organization (UNESCO) honored Yizhong with its Guillermo Cano World Press Freedom Prize in 2005. The award is named for Guillermo Cano, a Colombian journalist who was murdered in 1987 for reporting on the activities of powerful drug barons in South America.

"Censorship happens secretly; it is silent and effective," declares Yizhong. "By forbidding any paper evidence, and by phoning or sending text messages directly among different levels, only one-way communication takes place between the publicity department and the media leadership, and between higher- and lower-level media leaders. The only rule for subordinates is to be loyal to the higher leadership and not cause trouble for them. Accountability and respect have become more straightforward. In time, the media leadership and workers have become used to self-censorship. Members of staff can protect their jobs and personal interests by informing on and betraying others, and so this has become the principal management tool. The dark and dangerous sides of the human character have been exploited."[4]

Cheng Yizhong has become widely respected for his reporting on human rights violations. Yizhong was the editor in chief of *Nanfang Dushi Bao* (*Southern Metropolis Daily*) and *Xin Jing Bao* (*Beijing News*). Yizhong started out at the latter publication, sharing "forbidden news" in China. His stories included critical investigations of what life is really like in Chinese society. In 2003, Yizhong reported a story about a young graphic artist who had been killed in China. The young man was beaten to death while in police custody. As a result of the story, Yizhong and six of his coworkers were questioned by Guangzhou police in a corruption case.

One of the many organizations working to prevent censorship and improve access to official information worldwide is Article 19. The group is named for the Universal Declaration of Human Rights section that addresses freedom of expression. The organization has a vision of the future in which all people can speak their opinions, participate in decision-making, and make informed choices about their lives. As its website states, "People everywhere must be able to exercise their right to freedom of expression and their right to information. Without these rights, democracy, good governance, and development cannot happen."[5]

The Ultimate Prize

Journalist Anna Politkovskaya never shied away from controversy. Towards the end of her life, she had written numerous articles for the *Novaya Gazeta* about human rights violations in Chechnya. What she didn't know was that some of the biggest stories including her name would be about her murder. Politkovskaya had recently been working on a story about torture in that region when she was killed on an October afternoon in 2006. She had just returned to her apartment in Moscow, Russia, with some groceries.

Anna Politkovskaya

When Politkovskaya stepped into the elevator, a man wearing a baseball cap shot her four times. He had been waiting for her to get home. Politkovskaya was just forty-eight years old at the time.

Even though years have passed since the killing, Politkovskaya's murder remains unsolved. Four men from Chechnya and a former police officer will stand trial for the crime. Lom-Ali Gaitukayev has been charged with organizing the murder. His nephew, Rustam Makhmudov, is on trial for carrying it out. Makhmudov's two brothers have also been charged in the crime. The upcoming trial won't be the first for three of them who were acquitted in 2009.[6] But Russia's Supreme Court overturned that decision, paving the way for a new trial.

Lom-Ali Gaitukayev, Rustam Makhmudov, and Sergei Khadzhikurbanov are presently on trial for taking part in the murder of Anna Politkovskaya.

CHAPTER 3

Ending Discrimination

Human beings are discriminated against every day in places throughout the world. One person may be denied a certain freedom because of her race, ethnicity, or nationality. Another person might be victimized because of his sexual orientation. Other people might be discriminated against based on their gender, religion, or physical or mental disability. No circumstance makes discrimination okay. Every single person in the world is entitled to basic human rights.

A young, mentally-challenged Christian girl named Rimsha Masih was arrested in Pakistan for burning pages of the Koran in August of 2012. In this country, blasphemy, or disrespecting a religion, is against the law. Anyone who insults the Prophet Muhammad or defiles the Koran can be punished with twenty-five years in prison or even the death penalty. To make matters worse, many people falsely accuse members of religious minorities of this crime. In most cases the charges are eventually dropped when the police find that the claims are false. An investigation can take months, however. While it is underway, the accused person remains in jail. Families of those accused are often exposed to threats to their safety by religious extremists who take the law into their own hands.

Masih was finally freed in November of 2012. Her case made headlines all over the world when the police arrested the Muslim cleric who wrongfully accused her. Following an investigation into the matter, authorities charged Imam Khalid Jadoon Chishti with falsifying evidence against Masih. An arrest like this one was a rare event. While the arrest was a definite step in the right

Accused of insulting Islam, young Rimsha Masih spent three weeks in jail in 2012. In Pakistan, people found guilty of blasphemy can be imprisoned for twenty-five years. Even the death penalty is a legal punishment for the crime in the nation. Many people around the world—including certain Muslim leaders—spoke out against Masih's arrest and against her country's blasphemy laws in general. Wrongfully accused by a Muslim cleric, Masih was eventually freed. But the debate about Pakistan's blasphemy laws still rages on.

Rimsha Masih's arrest quickly became a topic of discussion in many places, including Islamabad, Pakistan. The subject of blasphemy and the country's laws pertaining to it evoke strong emotion from all sides of the issue. Here members of the Islamabad community meet at a local mosque to discuss the situation.

direction, Chishti was later acquitted when all the witnesses withdrew their testimony.

Masih's lawyer, Tahir Naveed, blames poor police procedure and pressure from Islamists for the disappointing outcome. "The court freed [Chishti] because the police failed to assure the witnesses that they would not be harmed," he explains. "Moreover, the trial court judges are also under immense pressure when hearing blasphemy cases."[1]

One of the witnesses was deputy mosque leader Hafiz Zubair. After telling the court that Chishti had placed burned pages into Masih's bag, he added, "I asked why he was fabricating the evidence. [Chishti] said this would ensure a strong case against the girl and would ultimately help them in evicting the Christians from the locality."[2] Before the case could be decided, though, Zubair and the six other witnesses changed their story. They then insisted that the police had forced them to lie about Chishti's actions.

Just before Masih was arrested, enraged neighbors surrounded her home. They demanded that police take action against her when a Muslim cleric accused her of burning pages of the Koran. As a Christian, Masih is in the religious minority in Pakistan. She and other Christians often live in fear of being mistreated for their beliefs.

Thankfully, some people in this religious majority are willing to stand up for what is right and not back down. The head of the Pakistan Ulema Council, a body of Islamic clerics, has offered the world some insight into the situation. Allama Tahir Ashrafi shares that just three days before all the witnesses began speaking of being pressured by the police, a rally was held in Rawalpindi. During the event extremists publicly threatened the witnesses, who then took back their original statements.

"Unfortunately, the extremist forces have once again proven their might," says Ashrafi. "I ask that if [Masih] was innocent and now [Chishti] has also been acquitted of the charge, who are the real faces behind this case? Shouldn't the trial court judge have asked police to unveil the perpetrators of the case? The fact is that everyone fears the extremist forces and are not ready to counter them."[3]

It is not unusual for religion to be a driving force behind discrimination. Things can get even more complicated, though,

Critics of the cleric who accused Rimsha Masih have spoken out, insisting that his motive was not merely upholding the law, but rather discouraging Christianity in Pakistan. Fortunately, some Pakistanis were also willing to speak up for Masih. One of them was Allama Tahir Ashrafi. An Islamic cleric and chairman of Pakistan Ulema Council, he called for a fair trial for the young Christian girl.

when religion becomes a tool for discriminating against a certain group of people. In Iran, for example, religious inequality between the genders has been written into the country's legislation. By law a woman must always be veiled when she is in public in

Iran. No such laws exist for Iranian men. It's not just a woman's physical appearance that is affected by the country's discriminatory treatment of the sexes. Women are also considered less reliable when it comes to the simple matter of telling the truth. In an Iranian court of law, a woman's testimony is "worth half of a man's."[4] This means that if a male witness calls a female witness a liar, it is his word that will be taken as the truth.

One of the most difficult parts of Iran's discriminatory laws is that they are based on Sharia, a set of laws that the religious leaders believe come directly from God. For this reason the leaders insist that the laws cannot be changed. But an Iranian journalist and activist named Parvin Ardalan is trying to do just that. "Islamic laws are not fixed," she counters. "Since the revolution, some articles have been changed; it is possible. Many laws are political rather than religious and it is up to the government if they want to change them."[5]

In 2006, Ardalan launched the One Million Signatures campaign. As the name implies, her goal is to get one million Iranians to demand a change for equal treatment of men and women under their country's laws. At first the plan was to share the signatures with Parliament. Ardalan and other women who are working on the campaign have decided to go in another direction, however. They realized that by passing the signatures on to the current Iranian government, they would be acknowledging its supreme power. Since that isn't something the women want to do, they are now thinking about passing the names on to the United Nations or a human rights organization instead.

When Ardalan participated in a protest against the election of Mahmoud Ahmedinejad, she discovered that her work had gone beyond a fight for women's rights. "What started as a protest against the election became a general protest for human rights. All the social and political movements were there: women, students, and different ethnic groups."[6]

Although her activism has forced her to live in exile in Sweden, Ardalan has no plans of giving up the fight for equal

Parvin Ardalan began by speaking out about women's rights in her native Iran. But her work has evolved into a fight for human rights in general. In 2007, Ardalan was named the recipient of the Olof Palme Prize in Stockholm, Sweden. Although the Iranian government tried to stop her from leaving the country, Ardalan now lives in Sweden, where she continues her activism.

rights in her home country. "The hope for change keeps me going. Sometimes I feel really tired, but I will never give up. I think it is good for us to try to realize our dreams. It makes me happy to see all the young women in the movement. They will be great leaders in Iranian society someday."[7]

Women in Rwanda

Women now serve in the governments of numerous countries around the world. Still, in most of these nations men outnumber the women by an overwhelming majority. One nation stands out, however. The central African country of Rwanda is the only nation in the entire world with a female majority in Parliament.

In 1994, the situation in Rwanda was anything but peaceful. In one of the bloodiest civil wars in history, more than eight hundred thousand people were killed in the country in just three months.[8] Fourteen years later, the country elected its first legislature consisting mostly of women.

Women not only hold the majority of seats in Parliament. They also occupy the seats of Speaker of Parliament and Supreme Court Chief. One-third of the cabinet is female as well.

Under this largely female leadership, Rwanda is thriving. Agnes Matilda Kalibata has served as minister of state in charge of agriculture. She shares, "Rwanda's economy has risen up from the genocide and prospered greatly on the backs of our women. Bringing women out of the home and fields has been essential to our rebuilding. In that process, Rwanda has changed forever. . . . We are becoming a nation that understands that there are huge financial benefits to equality."[9]

Dr. Agnes Kalibata (left) is Rwanda's Minister of Agriculture and Animal Resources. Margaret Mauwa is the Deputy Minister for Agriculture and Food Security of Malawi. The two leaders are seen here at the African Green Revolution Forum at the Accra International Conference Centre in Ghana.

CHAPTER 4

The Importance of Dignity and Education

Difficult circumstances often call for drastic measures. When natural disasters like earthquakes and hurricanes happen, people must work together to find solutions to problems that didn't even exist before the disaster struck. Faced with these desperate situations, people are often forced to abandon their normal ways of doing things in order to get through the crisis. No matter how dire the situation, however, one of the most important human rights that must be maintained is dignity.

When a devastating earthquake struck Haiti in January of 2010, organizations from around the world sent volunteers to the island nation. Instead of working with the local government, however, many of these groups began distributing aid on their own. While the intentions may have been good, the results were conditions that violated the basic elements of human rights. Months after the quake, a soccer field in the Solino neighborhood of Port-au-Prince was filled with camps for people who had been displaced by the disaster. More than six thousand people were living in the field outside a local church.[1] And no one appeared to be in charge.

Tents made from repurposed plastic and PVC pipes lined the field. These makeshift shelters were set so close to one another that there was little room to walk between them. When rain fell, muddy puddles formed. The mud was then tracked throughout the camp. The quality of life at the field proved to be even worse than the people's other options, but some of those options had been taken away. Twenty-three-year-old Sylvie Paul survived the quake only to be forced from her home by the United Nations

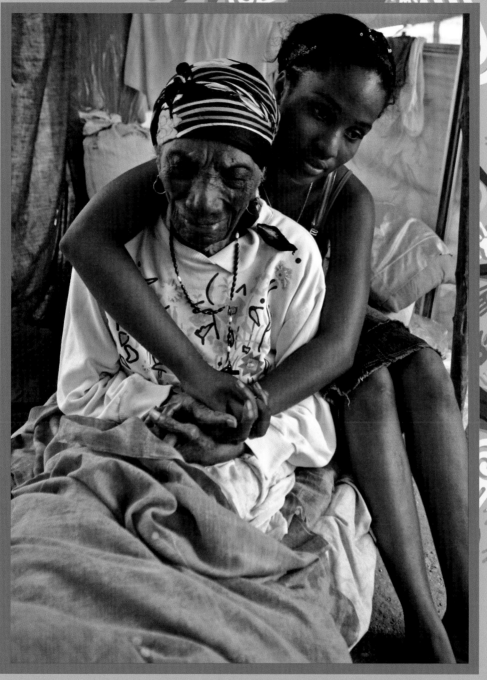

Thousands of Haitian people were forced to live in makeshift tents on a former soccer field following the 2010 earthquake in Port-au-Prince, Haiti. Two of them were seventeen-year-old Jenny Beamy Ais and her 109-year-old great-grandmother Frezilia Cetoute.

Stabilization Mission in Haiti (MINUSTAH). She recalls that the group destroyed her house, which had been located at the edge of the soccer field. "I would have rather stayed there where it was at least dry," she explains.[2]

It is possible that Paul's home was made unsafe by the earthquake, but the camp was proving to be unsafe in other ways. Much worse than the mud, the lack of bathrooms was causing a major threat to public health. The filthy conditions led to increased instances of fever and diseases like malaria and dengue. Some people at the camp traveled over a nearby ravine to use bathrooms in other campsites. But these bathrooms were so overused that they too were unsanitary. And in some cases, the people had to pay each time they used them.

Poor organization also affected the people's access to food. Humanitarian groups issued ration cards that could be exchanged for food, but there was little forewarning. Many people at the camp stayed up all night so they wouldn't miss their chance to feed their families. Nathalie Joseph is the mother of three children. She shares, "You can't afford to sleep when you hear that there's a card distribution. You never know where and when they will give it out. You just have to follow the noise of the crowd and hope you will get yours."[3]

Mark Schuller witnessed life in Haiti after the earthquake firsthand. He writes, "It is clear that the conditions of many of the settlements of displaced Haitians violate basic human dignity." He points out that a legal framework guaranteeing the social rights of displaced people was already in place when the earthquake occurred. "In 1998, the UN Office for Coordination for Humanitarian Affairs presented its Guiding Principles on Internal Displacement, which member states later ratified in 2005."[4] The document provides basic standards for health and hygiene, food and water, shelter, and sanitation.

The situation in Haiti is just one example of why we need to keep the fight for human rights going. The Guiding Principles on Internal Displacement was a great start, but the standards the document created must be enforced. Countries, both those

The United Nations Stabilization Mission brought emergency supplies to Port-au-Prince, Haiti following the January 2010 earthquake. Many Haitians traveled great distances to the distribution point so they could bring food back to their hungry families.

helping and those being helped, must understand the importance of honoring each person's dignity. That task is accomplished through education.

And speaking of education, it too is listed in the Universal Declaration of Human Rights. Article 26 states, "Education shall be directed to the full development of the human personality and to the strengthening of respect for human rights and fundamental freedoms. It shall promote understanding, tolerance, and friendship among all nations, racial or religious groups, and shall further the activities of the United Nations for the maintenance of peace."[5]

One organization that is helping to make education accessible to all is Libraries Without Borders (LWB). The mission of the nonprofit organization is to make information resources more accessible to everyone. It works to build and grow libraries in developing regions throughout the world. When the 2010

earthquake occurred in Haiti, LWB sent an emergency mission to the country.

Patrick Weil is the chairman and founder of LWB. He states, "Access to books, culture, and knowledge for victims of natural and man-made disasters is important because these allow

Even in the midst of great tragedy—and sometimes because of it—people need to keep their minds busy. Libraries Without Borders works to fill this role in areas of the world dealing with immense challenges like the earthquake in Haiti. To the Haitian children, the "BiblioTaptap" is much more than just a van. The arrival of this library on wheels means access to books, public readings, and just as importantly, a pleasant distraction as their families work to rebuild their lives.

individuals to reconnect with the rest of humanity and provide them the strength to look toward the future. . . . We believe also that such education efforts beyond formal schools, such as mini-libraries in disaster zones and storytime programs for displaced persons, must be made a priority, because they cultivate the human spirit and provide distractions to help disaster victims cope with trauma."[6]

Some people in Europe and the United States questioned whether access to books was really that important in light of all the other things the Haitians needed. This reaction surprised Weil. He responds, "Since Libraries Without Borders believes that dignity through books, writing, and learning should not be denied to victims of humanitarian disasters, we have placed greater emphasis in our projects on providing relief services."[7]

LWB has built or supported seventy-four school and university libraries, twenty-eight public libraries, and thirty-one special libraries throughout Haiti. These include prison libraries, law libraries, and libraries for women's rights. Equally important, the group has trained nearly two hundred Haitians as librarians, so the work that was started can continue long after the most troubling times are over.

Weil hopes that LWB can teach the world that education is part of human dignity. "Believing strongly that dignity through books, writing, and learning should not be denied to victims of humanitarian disasters, Libraries Without Borders is calling on international organizations and governments to better take into consideration the role these play in emergency situations. Reading and expression must take their place among food, water, shelter, and health as basic needs and priorities in humanitarian emergencies."[8]

Education Helps People Help Themselves

Education is a very special human right in that it builds on itself. When children and adults are given access to education, their lives improve in numerous ways. An educated person living in poverty has a better chance of finding a higher-paying job. Learning about the workings of government can help a person get involved in the political process and make changes. Perhaps most importantly, education helps people understand that things can change. Learning about other people who have overcome similar situations gives people hope.

Education also helps people make an important difference in the lives of others. For example, many poor areas of the world struggle with widespread disease. When just a few people learn how to stop diseases from spreading, they can then pass this knowledge on to others. The students become the teachers, improving the lives of everyone around them.

In many parts of the world, people who are denied basic human rights do not realize that things *should* change. They know their lives are hard, but they do the best they can to deal with the challenges before them. When people learn that they are entitled to freedom, equality, and nonviolence, it sets them on the path to making these rights a reality. Education makes other human rights possible.

United States Secretary of Education Arne Duncan visits a school in Haiti.

CHAPTER 5

Enforcing Human Rights Laws

By itself the phrase "human rights" does very little. Without enforcement, even national or international laws that support these rights cannot protect a person who is being mistreated. Convincing certain national governments to pass human rights laws can be extremely difficult. Creating a complete list of international laws that do not contradict the beliefs of any nations can be even more challenging. Certainly, the problem cannot be solved overnight. But as we consider the best course of action, people are struggling to survive amidst abuses most of us can hardly imagine.

In many developing regions, one of the biggest impediments to human rights is the police department itself. Corruption quickly trickles down from high-level government officials to those who work in law enforcement. In these areas one of two things often happen when the people go to the police for help: Either they are ignored, or the problem worsens. Dishonest and brutally violent police officers are common in certain areas of the world.

In a 2010 article in *The New Yorker* magazine, William Finnegan states, "Although organized crime requires corruption at all levels of government to function effectively, the cop on the beat is a crucial piece of the machinery. Police officers can provide key information and services. In Mexico, they often moonlight for the cartels as drivers, bodyguards, kidnappers, hit men, drug runners, lookouts, thieves, corpse-disposal experts, and extortionists. Their uniforms come in handy on raids, robberies, kidnappings."[1] He adds that many cops are also paid to look the other way when

United States citizen Yanira Maldonado is seen here with her husband Gary shortly after her release from a Mexican prison. The forty-two-year-old wife and mother of seven came to Mexico for a relative's funeral. But while there, she was accused of smuggling twelve pounds of marijuana. Video footage of the couple as they boarded their bus proved that she couldn't have committed the crime.

crimes take place, pretending to see and hear nothing at all. Others lie about what they have seen, blaming crimes on innocent people.

Even in countries where corruption is widespread, honest law enforcement officials do exist. Retired Lieutenant Colonel Julian Leyzaola Perez was the chief of police in Tijuana, Mexico, until 2008. At that time he was promoted to Tijuana's secretary of public security. His new title soon led to offers of bribes from some high-level criminals. Once, a former Army colleague asked to meet with him. At first Perez thought the man wanted a job.

Fortunately, some members of Mexican law enforcement are honest. Retired Lieutenant Colonel Julian Leyzaola Perez had his work cut out for him as the chief of police in Tijuana, Mexico. Because of his diligent work to rid the city of drug gangs, he was later named Tijuana's Secretary of Public Security. He would rise to this challenge as well.

In 2014, Mexican President Enrique Pena Nieto announced the capture of Joaquin Guzman Loera (shown below). Known as El Chapo, Guzman was considered one of the most wanted drug lords in the world. Lieutenant Colonel Julian Leyzaola Perez's former friend and fellow Army serviceman worked for Guzman. The former colleague tried to recruit Perez onto Guzman's payroll. But Perez refused. He wanted to capture Guzman instead.

Chapter 5

But as it turned out, he already had one, working for a well-known drug lord known as Chapo Guzman.

Perez remembers, "He said, 'I'm not looking for a job. I am here as an ambassador for Chapo Guzman. He wants to pay you eighty thousand dollars a week to go to conferences and meetings, to set up sister-city programs.' He wanted to pay me, in other words," Perez explains, "to stop doing my job."[2] Perez told the man he was a traitor and proceeded to escort him to the attorney general's office to inform the department about the offer.

The poorer the people whose rights have been violated, the more difficult it usually is for them to get the help they need. One of the biggest human rights problems is the unfair treatment of people accused of crimes in certain countries. Many developing countries have few lawyers. The United States has one lawyer for

every 749 people. Zambia, on the other hand, has one lawyer for every 25,667 people.[3] A severe lack of prosecutors in particular makes the problem even worse. When a person is accused of a crime, he or she has little hope of a speedy trial.

In India, a shortage of judges makes a prompt trial almost impossible. With only eleven judges for every one million people, defendants can wait many years until their case can even be heard in a court of law. With more than thirty million cases awaiting trial, cases remain open for fifteen years, on average. Even before trial dates are set, some people actually spend more time in jail than the maximum amount of time that the crimes they are charged with carry.[4]

Even though they are gradual, important changes are taking place. The International Justice Mission (IJM), for example, has

Even children celebrated the end of Moammar Gaddhafi's regime in 2011. The military compound known as Baba al Azizia in Tripoli, Libya, quickly became a tourist attraction. Today it is a symbol for the important changes that took place following the leader's ousting. Gaddhafi had kept the compound hidden from the rest of the world while he was in power. Public access to it marked the beginning of change in the area.

created a promising model for reform. Called collaborative casework, it requires human rights lawyers and law enforcement to work together with local authorities. For this reason it works best in places where national and local governments are willing to make the necessary changes. The lawyers, police, and local officials can identify victims of human rights abuse, remove them from their violent situations, and work to prosecute the responsible parties. The IJM has used this approach to prosecute thousands of cases of human rights violations against the poor over the last decade.

Small changes could be a promising sign of the way the world will view human rights in the future. In March of 2011, the United Nations Security Council voted to approve a no-fly zone over Libya to keep Moammar Gaddhafi from performing aerial attacks on his own people. When it came time for the vote, both China and Russia chose to abstain, or not vote on the matter.[5] This was a huge step forward for both nations, as they normally do not approve military intervention on what they consider internal matters. If they had chosen to use their vetoes, they could have blocked the resolution.

Another example of progress, however small, occurred that same year in November. The Arab League voted to impose economic sanctions on Syria due to the country's violent attacks against protesters.[6] Both the European Union and the United States had previously imposed sanctions on the country as well. But this was the first time that the Arab League had taken such a measure against one of its member states.

Many things will affect the way the world views human rights in the future. Emerging powers like China and Russia, as well as India and Turkey, could play a big role in this process. Technology could have a profound effect on the way we view human rights as well. Even the middle class and whether it continues to grow—and care about human rights—will have a big impact. Who will make the biggest difference in the protection of human rights, after all, are the human beings demanding to be heard.

The Situation in Syria

The fight for human rights is at the center of a brutal civil war currently taking place in Syria. The violence in the Middle Eastern country began in March of 2011. At that time fifteen children were arrested for painting anti-government graffiti on walls in the city of Deraa. Reports of their torture soon began spreading across the world as protestors took to the streets. Acting peacefully, the Syrian citizens were demanding two things. First, they wanted the mistreated young people released. Second, they wanted changes made to the Syrian government. These changes would end human rights violations in the country.

President Bashar al-Assad and his government responded with violence. The Syrian army opened fire on the protestors. They killed four people in the process. Following the brutal assault, the army then shot at people who attended the funerals of those who had been killed. Another innocent person was killed in the process.

Many people responded by demanding that al-Assad resign. When he refused, the conflict worsened, and eventually, it turned into an outright civil war. Since the fighting began, the death toll has risen to more

The civil war in Syria began in 2011 when the government responded to citizen protests with arrests and censorship. Instead of trying to solve the issues that the people were speaking out against, the Syrian government made them worse by further violating human rights. Police brutality and the torture of prisoners caused the situation to intensify. What began as protests in the city of Deraa quickly spread across the country. Although the government has released hundreds of political prisoners, the fight for a government that respects human rights continues. The situation has gained attention from numerous other countries, including the United States.

than one hundred thousand people.[7] In August of 2013, journalists began reporting that al-Assad had used chemical weapons in an attack on rebel forces near the capital city of Damascus. The use of chemical weapons is banned under international law. At the time of this printing, several countries including the United States are considering what they should do to help the Syrian people.

WHAT YOU CAN DO TO HELP

Even though you may live far away from the areas where the worst human rights violations are happening, you can make a difference. Here are a few ways that you can help:

Educate yourself about human rights. Visit websites like Youth for Human Rights to learn about the violations that are happening right now and what young people can do to improve the situation: http://www.youthforhumanrights.org/take-action.html

Write letters to your local government representatives about the problem of human rights. Tell these people how important it is for them to get involved in the fight.

Write a letter to the editor of your local newspaper (or a national one) about human rights to help call attention to the problem. Education is the first step to ensuring that human rights are respected throughout the world.

Donate part of your allowance or some of the money you make at a part-time job to a reputable organization such as Amnesty International, Human Rights Watch, etc.

Talk to your family members, friends, and classmates about getting involved, or use social media to get your message out. By spreading the word about the need for change, you turn one voice into many.

CHAPTER NOTES

Introduction

1. United Nations, *The Universal Declaration of Human Rights*. http://www.un.org/en/documents/udhr/

2. Louis Charbonneau, Reuters, "Syria, Iran to Run for U.N. Human Rights Council: Envoys," July 10, 2013. http://www.unwatch.org/site/apps/nlnet/content2.aspx?c=bdKKISNqEmG&b=1319279&ct=13219747

Chapter 1

1. Beth Thomas Hertz, *Ophthalmology Times*, "African Teen Has New Vision on Life," November 1, 2011, p. 6.

2. John Jessup, CBN News, "'Lost Boy' Begs US to Help End Sudan Slave Trade," October 9, 2011. http://www.cbn.com/cbnnews/world/2011/October/Lost-Boy-Begs-US-to-Help-End-Sudan-Slave-Trade/

3. Ibid.

4. Julie Bindel, *New Statesman*, "A Weapon Against Half the World," March 5, 2010, p. 38.

5. Ibid.

6. SouthAfrica.info, "The Constitution of South Africa." http://www.southafrica.info/about/democracy/constitution.htm#.UienUevD8qQ

7. CEDAW 2013, "Frequently Asked Questions." http://www.cedaw2011.org/index.php/about-cedaw/faq

8. CEDAW 2013, "What's in It for US." http://www.cedaw2011.org/index.php/whats-in-it-for-us

9. United Nations, *The Universal Declaration of Human Rights*. http://www.un.org/en/documents/udhr/

10. Ueslei Marcelino, Reuters, "EU Lawmakers Nominate Snowden for Sakharov Human Rights Prize," September 12, 2013. http://rt.com/news/snowden-sakharov-prize-freedom-eu-737/

Chapter 2

1. United Nations, The Universal Declaration of Human Rights. http://www.un.org/en/documents/udhr/

2. Martha Cruz, *Americas*, "Freedom of Expression: Catalina Botero," January/February 2012, Volume 64, Issue 1, p. 30.

3. Ibid.

4. Cheng Yizhong, *New Statesman*, "The Virus of Censorship," October 19-25, 2012, p. 4.

5. Article 19, "What We Do." http://www.article19.org/pages/en/what-we-do.html

6. Shaun Walker, *The Independent*, "Chechens Face Second Trial in Anna Politkovskaya Murder Case," June 20, 2013. http://www.independent.co.uk/news/world/europe/chechens-face-second-trial-in-anna-politkovskaya-murder-case-8667415.html

Chapter 3

1. *Morning Star News*, "Imam in Pakistan Acquitted of Desecrating Koran, Framing Christian Girl for 'Blasphemy,'" August 18, 2013. http://morningstarnews.org/2013/08/imam-acquitted-of-desecrating-koran-framing-christian-girl-for-blasphemy/

2. Melissa Steffan, *Christianity Today*, "Another Surprise Twist in Pakistan's 'Turning Point' Blasphemy Case," August 19, 2013. http://www.christianitytoday.com/gleanings/2012/september/surprise-twist-in-pakistan-blasphemy-case-rimsha-masih.html

3. *Morning Star News*, "Imam in Pakistan Acquitted of Desecrating Koran, Framing Christian Girl for 'Blasphemy,'" August 18, 2013. http://morningstarnews.org/2013/08/imam-acquitted-of-desecrating-koran-framing-christian-girl-for-blasphemy/

4. Jenny Cleveson, *New Internationalist Magazine*, "Interview with Parvin Ardalan," March 2011, Issue 440, p. 46.

5. Ibid.

6. Ibid.

7. Ibid.

8. Palash Ghosh, *International Business Times*, "Rwanda: The Only Government in the World Dominated by Women," January 3, 2012. http://www.ibtimes.com/rwanda-only-government-world-dominated-women-213623

9. Ibid.

CHAPTER NOTES

Chapter 4

1. Mark Schuller, *NACLA Report on the Americas*, "Shattered and Scattered: Haiti's Quake Through the Lens of Human Rights," July/August 2010, Volume 43, Issue 4, p. 20.
2. Ibid.
3. Ibid.
4. Ibid.
5. United Nations, *The Universal Declaration of Human Rights*. http://www.un.org/en/documents/udhr/
6. Leonard Kniffel, *American Libraries*, "Disaster Relief . . . with Books," May 2013, Volume 44, Issue 5, p. 30.
7. Ibid.
8. Ibid., p. 32.

Chapter 5

1. William Finnegan, *The New Yorker*, "In the Name of the Law," October 18, 2010.
2. Ibid.
3. Gary Haugen and Victor Boutros, *Foreign Affairs*, "And Justice For All," May/June 2010, Volume 89, Issue 3, p. 51-62.
4. Ibid.
5. Josh Calder, *The Futurist*, "Who Will Be Free? The Battles for Human Rights to 2050," November/December 2012, Volume 46, Issue 6, p. 29.
6. Ibid.
7. BBC, "What's Happening in Syria and Will the Violence End?" August 27, 2013. http://www.bbc.co.uk/newsround/16979186

FURTHER READING

Books

King, Martin Luther. *Why We Can't Wait.* Boston, Massachusetts: Beacon Press, 2011.

Mandela, Nelson. *Conversations with Myself.* New York: Farrar, Straus and Giroux, 2010.

Merino, Faith. *Human Rights.* New York: Facts on File, Inc., 2011.

On the Internet

American Civil Liberties Union: Human Rights
https://www.aclu.org/human-rights

Amnesty International: Learn About Human Rights
http://www.amnesty.org/en/human-rights

Amnesty International: Respect My Rights
http://respectmyrights.org/

Human Rights Watch
http://www.hrw.org/

United Nations: Human Rights
http://www.un.org/en/rights/

YouTube: The Human Rights Channel
http://www.youtube.com/user/Humanrights

Works Consulted

Article 19. "What We Do."
http://www.article19.org/pages/en/what-we-do.html

BBC. "What's Happening in Syria and Will the Violence End?" August 27, 2013. http://www.bbc.co.uk/newsround/16979186

Benhabib, Seyla. *Dignity in Adversity: Human Rights in Turbulent Times.* Cambridge, UK: Polity Press, 2011.

Bindel, Julie. "A Weapon Against Half the World." *New Statesman*, March 5, 2010, p. 38.

Calder, Josh. "Who Will Be Free? The Battles for Human Rights to 2050." *The Futurist*, November/December 2012, Volume 46, Issue 6, p. 29.

CEDAW 2013. "Frequently Asked Questions." http://www.cedaw2011.org/index.php/about-cedaw/faq

CEDAW 2013. "What's in It for US." http://www.cedaw2011.org/index.php/whats-in-it-for-us

FURTHER READING

Charbonneau, Louis. "Syria, Iran to Run for U.N. Human Rights Council: Envoys." Reuters, July 10, 2013. http://www.unwatch.org/site/apps/nlnet/content2.aspx?c=bdKKISNqEmG&b=1319279&ct=13219747

Cleveson, Jenny. "Interview with Parvin Ardalan." *New Internationalist Magazine*, March 2011, Issue 440, p. 46.

Cruz, Martha. "Freedom of Expression: Catalina Botero." *Americas*, January/February 2012, Volume 64, Issue 1, p. 30.

Fagan, Andrew. *The Atlas of Human Rights: Mapping Violations of Freedom Around the Globe*. Berkeley, California: University of California Press, 2010.

Finnegan, William. "In the Name of the Law." *The New Yorker*, October 18, 2010.

Gessen, Keith. "The Accused." *The New Yorker*, March 23, 2009.

Ghosh, Palash. "Rwanda: The Only Government in the World Dominated by Women." *International Business Times*, January 3, 2012. http://www.ibtimes.com/rwanda-only-government-world-dominated-women-213623

Haugen, Gary, and Victor Boutros. "And Justice For All." *Foreign Affairs*, May/June 2010, Volume 89, Issue 3, p. 51-62.

Hertz, Beth Thomas. "African Teen Has New Vision on Life." *Ophthalmology Times*, November 1, 2011, p. 6.

Jessup, John. "'Lost Boy' Begs US to Help End Sudan Slave Trade." CBN News, October 9, 2011. http://www.cbn.com/cbnnews/world/2011/October/Lost-Boy-Begs-US-to-Help-End-Sudan-Slave-Trade/

Kniffel, Leonard. "Disaster Relief . . . with Books." *American Libraries*, May 2013, Volume 44, Issue 5, p. 30.

MacFarquhar, Neil, and Nada Bakri. "Isolating Syria, Arab League Imposes Broad Sanctions." *The New York Times*, November 27, 2011. http://www.nytimes.com/2011/11/28/world/middleeast/arab-league-prepares-to-vote-on-syrian-sanctions.html?pagewanted=all&_r=0

Marcelino, Ueslei. "EU Lawmakers Nominate Snowden for Sakharov Human Rights Prize." Reuters, September 12, 2013. http://rt.com/news/snowden-sakharov-prize-freedom-eu-737/

Merino, Faith. *Human Rights*. New York: Facts on File, Inc., 2011.

Morning Star News. "Imam in Pakistan Acquitted of Desecrating Koran, Framing Christian Girl for 'Blasphemy.'" August 18, 2013. http://morningstarnews.org/2013/08/imam-acquitted-of-desecrating-koran-framing-christian-girl-for-blasphemy/

Reilly, Niamh. *Women's Human Rights*. Cambridge, England: Polity Press, 2010.

Roth, Kenneth. *Human Rights Watch: World Report 2013*. New York: Seven Stories Press, 2013.

Schuller, Mark. "Shattered and Scattered: Haiti's Quake Through the Lens of Human Rights." *NACLA Report on the Americas*, July/August 2010, Volume 43, Issue 4, p. 20.

SouthAfrica.info. "The Constitution of South Africa." http://www.southafrica.info/about/democracy/constitution.htm#.UienUevD8qQ

Steffan, Melissa. "Another Surprise Twist in Pakistan's 'Turning Point' Blasphemy Case." *Christianity Today*, August 19, 2013. http://www.christianitytoday.com/gleanings/2012/september/surprise-twist-in-pakistan-blasphemy-case-rimsha-masih.html

United Nations. The Universal Declaration of Human Rights. http://www.un.org/en/documents/udhr/

Walker, Shaun. "Chechens Face Second Trial in Anna Politkovskaya Murder Case." *The Independent*, June 20, 2013. http://www.independent.co.uk/news/world/europe/chechens-face-second-trial-in-anna-politkovskaya-murder-case-8667415.html

Yizhong, Cheng. "The Virus of Censorship." *New Statesman*, October 19-25, 2012, p. 4.

GLOSSARY

apartheid (uh-PAHRT-heyt)—Segregation of the nonwhite population by law in South Africa from 1948 until 1994.

acquit (uh-KWIT)—To declare not guilty.

baron (BAR-uhn)—Someone with great power in a particular field.

blasphemy (BLAS-fuh-mee)—Disrespect of a religion or anything held sacred.

corrupt (kuh-RUHPT)—Guilty of dishonest practices.

defile (dih-FAHYL)—To taint or dishonor.

dengue (DENG-gee)—An infectious fever that occurs in warm climates, characterized by joint and muscle pain.

discriminate (dih-SKRIM-uh-neyt)—To make a judgment for or against a person on the basis of the group, class, or category to which the person belongs.

dissident (DIS-i-duhnt)—A person who disagrees.

epidemic (ep-i-DEM-ik)—A rapid spread in the occurrence of something unpleasant.

exile (EG-zahyl)—Expulsion from one's homeland by law.

humanitarianism (hyoo-man-i-TAIR-ee-uh-niz-uhm)—The practice of helping to improve the welfare and happiness of people.

malaria (muh-LAIR-ee-uh)—A disease characterized by chills, fever, and sweating.

minority (mi-NAWR-i-tee)—An group of people forming less than half of the whole.

oppressed (uh-PREST)—Burdened with cruel or unjust restraints.

rapporteur (rap-awr-TUR)—A person who compiles and presents official reports.

ratification (rat-uh-fi-KEHY-shuhn)—The act of confirming officially.

ravine (ruh-VEEN)—A narrow valley with steep sides formed by water erosion.

sanction (SANGK-shuhn)—A penalty for disobedience enacted by the law of one state against another state.

stigma (STIG-muh)—Disgrace for having done something that is socially unacceptable.

subordinate (suh-BAWR-dn-it)—A person of a lower order or rank.

tyrannical (ti-RAN-i-kuhl)—Overly cruel or harsh.

vigilant (VIJ-uh-luhnt)—Always watching to detect danger.

INDEX

Ahmedinejad, Mahmoud 23

al-Assad, Bashar 41

Amnesty International 9–10, 42

apartheid 9

Arab League 40

Ardalan, Parvin 23–24

Article 19 16

Begum, Rasheeda 10

blasphemy 18–21, 22

Botero, Catalina 14–15

Cano, Guillermo 15

Chechnya 17

China 5, 11, 15–16, 40
  Beijing 15–16
  Hong Kong 11

Chishti, Khalid Jadoon 18–21, 22

Christian Solidarity International 6–8

Colombia 15

Convention on the Elimination of All Forms of Discrimination Against Women 9–10

Deng, Ker Aleu 6–8

drugs 15, 34, 35, 36–38

Eibner, John 8

Gaddhafi, Moammar 38–39, 40

Guiding Principles on Internal Displacement 28

Guillermo Cano World Press Freedom Prize 15

Guzman Loera, Joaquin ("El Chapo") 37, 38

Haiti 26–32, 33
  Port-au-Prince 26

Haller, Julia 7, 8

human rights and violations
  abuse (physical) 6
  dignity 4–5, 26–32
  education 5, 29–33, 42
  equality/discrimination 6, 8–10, 18–25

gender 8, 9–10, 21–25
race 9
religion 18–21

expression, speech, opinion/censorship 12–17, 41

food 28, 29

freedom 6–10

government/police corruption 14, 15, 16, 34–41

health care/disease 5, 28, 33

housing/shelter 26–29

justice 35, 38–40

murder 14, 17

organized crime 14, 34, 36–38

privacy 11

religion 5, 18–23, 29

slavery 6–8

voting 5, 6

Human Rights Watch 5, 42

India 39, 40

International Covenant on Civil and Political Rights 5

International Covenant on Economical, Social, and Cultural Rights 5

International Justice Mission 39–40

Iran 5, 10, 22–24

Joseph, Nathalie 28

Justice For Women 9

Kalibata, Agnes Matilda 25

Libraries Without Borders 30–32

Libya 38–39, 40
  Tripoli 38–39

Maldonado, Yanira 35

Masih, Rimsha 18–21, 22

Mexico 14, 34, 35, 36–38
  Tijuana 36–38

National Security Agency (NSA) 11

natural disasters 26–32

news reporting 12, 14–16, 17, 42

Olof Palme Prize 24

Pakistan 9, 10, 18–21, 22
  Islamabad 20–21

Paul, Sylvie 26, 28

Pena Nieto, Enrique 37

Perez, Julian Leyzaola 36–38

Politkovskaya, Anna 17

Roosevelt, Eleanor 13

Russia 5, 17, 40

Rwanda 25

Sakharov Prize 11

Snowden, Edward 11

South Africa 9

South Sudan 7, 8, 10

Sudan 6–8, 10

Sweden 23–24

Syria 5, 40–41
  Damascus 41
  Deraa 41

technology 11, 40

Thirteenth Amendment 6

Turkey 9, 30

United Kingdom 9

United Nations 4–5, 13, 15, 23, 26, 28, 29, 40
  Commission on Human Rights 13
  Educational, Scientific, and Cultural Organization (UNESCO) 15
  Human Rights Control 5
  Security Council 40
  Stabilization Mission in Haiti 26, 28, 29

United States 4, 6–8, 10, 11, 12, 13, 32, 33, 38–39, 40, 42

Universal Declaration of Human Rights 4–5, 11, 12, 13, 16, 29

Weil, Patrick 31–32

Yizhong, Cheng 15–16

Zambia 39

ABOUT THE AUTHOR

Tammy Gagne is the author of numerous books for adults and children, including *Life on the Reservations* and *Your Guide to Becoming a US Citizen* for Mitchell Lane Publishers. She resides in northern New England with her husband and son. One of her favorite pastimes is visiting schools to speak to kids about the writing process.